... . WHAT'S AT ISSUE? ....

PREJUDICE & DIFFERENCE

Paul Wignall

Heinemann
LIBRARY

H **www.heinemann.co.uk**
Visit our website to find out more information about **Heinemann Library** books.

To order:
☎ Phone 44 (0) 1865 888066
📄 Send a fax to 44 (0) 1865 314091
💻 Visit the Heinemann Bookshop at www.heinemann.co.uk to browse our catalogue and order online.

First published in Great Britain by Heinemann Library, Halley Court, Jordan Hill, Oxford OX2 8EJ, a division of Reed Educational and Professional Publishing Ltd. Heinemann is a registered trademark of Reed Educational & Professional Publishing Limited.

OXFORD MELBOURNE AUCKLAND JOHANNESBURG BLANTYRE
GABORONE IBADAN PORTSMOUTH NH (USA) CHICAGO

Designed by Tinstar Design (www.tinstar.co.uk)
Illustrations by Nicholas Beresford-Davies
Originated by Ambassador Litho Ltd
Printed in Hong Kong/China

ISBN 0 431 03542 3

04 03 02 01 00
10 9 8 7 6 5 4 3 2 1

British Library Cataloguing in Publication Data
Wignall, Paul
      Prejudice and difference. – (What's at issue?)
      1. Prejudices – Juvenile literature 2. Individual differences – Juvenile literature
      I. Title
      303.3'85

Acknowledgements
The publishers would like to thank the following for permission to reproduce photographs:
Associated Press: p11, p33; Childline: p40; Corbis: pp7,8, 19, 20, 24, 25, 26, 30, 32, 34, 35, 36, 39, 43, Penny Tweedie p14, Joseph Sohm p17, Michael St Maur Sheil p22, David H Wells p23, Sergio Dorantes p38; DfEE: p12; Heinemann: pp9, 27; Hulton Getty: pp4, 42; PA News: p29; Photodisc: p41; Popperfoto p31; Photofusion p29; Rex Features: p21; The Stock Market: pp13, 16; Tony Stone Images: Graeme Harris p10, Tony May p15; Wiener Forman: p5

Cover photograph: Hutchison Library: Crispin Hughes.

Our thanks to Julie Turner (School Counsellor, Banbury School, Oxfordshire) for her comments in the preparation of this book.

Every effort has been made to contact copyright holders of any material reproduced in this book. Any omissions will be rectified in subsequent printings if notice is given to the Publisher.

Any words appearing in the text in bold, **like this**, are explained in the Glossary.

Contents

Introduction

Differences are a fact of human life. And yet those very differences can become the source of unhappiness, **oppression** and persecution. They can even become matters of life and death. Can it ever be right to treat people badly just because of the colour of their skin, because of their religious beliefs or sexual orientation, or because they are women or children? In this book you will see how prejudices like these affect the lives of many people. How can we create a society where prejudice and **discrimination** have no place, and where the differences between people are celebrated and enjoyed? In this book you will have a chance to answer these questions for yourself.

What is prejudice?

Difference

No one is completely like anyone else. We are all individuals with our own characteristics, attitudes, likes and dislikes, hopes and fears. Here are a few examples. Some people write with their right hand, others with their left. Some people speak Welsh, some Punjabi, some English, and so on. Some people are young, some are old. Some are rich, some are poor. Some are male, some are female. Some people's skin has one particular **pigmentation**, other people's has another.

Differences like these are simply facts of life, and yet at one time or another they have all been the cause of ill-treatment, or harassment, or even persecution of one group by another. Today, no teacher will be concerned about whether you write with your right or your left hand. However, even 50 years ago, some left-handed children had their left hands tied behind their backs and were made to write with their right hand.

Today, Welsh is taught in Welsh schools, but 100 years ago the British government encouraged teachers to try to stamp out the Welsh language. Children caught speaking Welsh had a board hung round their neck with the letters 'WN' on it – 'Welsh Not'. At the end of the day, the child who was wearing the board was punished with a severe beating.

Soldiers hiding from a camera during race disturbances in the USA.

Until recently, women were not allowed into the pavilion at Lord's, the cricket ground in London. Some golf clubs have tried to prevent Jews or people who were deemed 'socially inferior' from becoming members. From time to time, there are allegations that people are not promoted or given pay rises because they come from the black community, or are women.

Difference is a fact of human life. And yet those very differences can become a source of unhappiness, **oppression** and persecution. They can even become matters of life and death.

PREJUDICE – WHAT IS IT?

The word 'prejudice' comes from two Latin words, *pre* ('before') and *judicium* ('trial' or 'sentence'). It originally meant information known about someone that would put them at a disadvantage in a court of law. It is an important principle of justice that everyone should have **equality** in court, and that judges should make decisions based on the facts before them – they should not 'pre-judge' or be prejudiced.

We might say that not pre-judging people is an important principle in everyday life too. But sometimes decisions are made for other reasons, because of, say, the colour of someone's skin, or how they speak, or what they look like. Decisions like these are the result of prejudice. They are made when we have formed opinions about people and things that are not based on knowledge or understanding, not on the 'facts in front of us', but for other, more **superficial** reasons.

Personal and institutional prejudice

Prejudice can take many forms. Some people may be deliberately prejudiced. Their attitudes to others are conscious and they go out of their way to express them, as, for example, so-called neo-Nazi groups who whip up hatred against people from black or Jewish communities.

But many of us have prejudices simply because they are a part of our society, or the particular bit of society to which we belong. Prejudices can have an important, though negative, part to play in keeping a group together. A prejudice allows one group to dominate another. It can be like glue, helping some people stick together.

We probably all have prejudices of one sort or another, but as we grow up and take our place in the adult world it is important that we understand what our own negative opinions are, and do our best to get rid of them.

'The Jewish teacher and their children are expelled from the school' – an illustration from a German school book of 1938. Within seven years nearly six million Jews would be killed in Nazi-dominated Europe.

5

What causes prejudice?

Prejudice thrives on ignorance and anxiety. It begins when we make assumptions about other people, based on just one or two of their characteristics.

Who am I?

Try this – on a sheet of paper, create the fullest description of yourself that you can. Where were you born? Where do you live now? What do you look like? Are you a girl or a boy? Are you left-handed or right-handed? What languages do you speak? Do not leave out anything, however unimportant it might seem, and it will not be long before you have filled your sheet of paper. Now take another one, and in the middle, draw a circle. That's you. Put your name inside. Now draw other circles on the paper. They are all the people in your life. Put their names inside the circles. Now draw lines connecting those circles to your circle, and lines connecting the various circles to each other, and label the lines to indicate the relationship – 'parent', 'teacher' and so on. That page will be quite full too. Look at the two pages. You are a complex person, with many characteristics, living in the middle of a whole network of different relationships. Everyone else in the world is just the same.

Prejudice rules when we define a whole and complex person by just one or two characteristics. It rules when we decide that someone is simply 'gay' or 'blind' or 'black' or 'Roman Catholic' or 'fat' or 'wears glasses', and forget that they are many other things too. The picture we then have becomes a **caricature** – a picture that distorts the truth about someone, and allows us to stop treating them as human beings and start treating them as things.

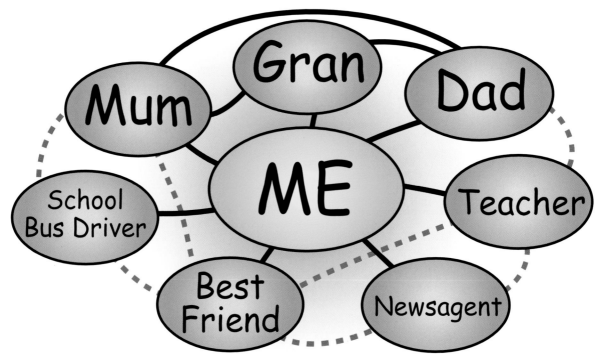

● *One example of prejudice overwhelming a society is the way in which the leaders of Nazi Germany in the 1930s were able to channel people's anxieties about unemployment and poverty into greater hatred of the Jews. A long-standing suspicion that the Jewish community was wealthy was fed with so-called 'facts' about Jewish bankers and shopkeepers. As these 'facts' were increasingly believed, so the authorities encouraged attacks on Jewish property and also passed laws removing Jews' **rights** to protection, or education, and preventing them from playing any part in society. So-called 'scientific' attempts were even made to define Jews as less than fully human. These 'reasons' and 'facts' then justified more hatred and **oppression**, leading to the murder of nearly six million Jews, rich and poor, old and young, between 1939 and 1945.*

Segregation by law has only been banned in the US since the mid-1960s. In other countries, for example South Africa, **apartheid** was still in place until the early 1990s.

THE CYCLE OF PREJUDICE

Prejudices are opinions we form about other people, which help to justify our own anxieties or fears and which are based on inadequate or distorted facts. Prejudice is closely linked to power. Individuals or groups who feel their power is under threat try to protect themselves by treating minority groups as inferior, as unequal. They begin to discriminate against them – refusing to give them jobs, for instance. This **discrimination** quickly leads on to oppression, in which the majority group totally dominates the minority, refusing them access to any of the good things society can offer – education, health care, decent housing, and so on. Finally, oppression leads to **repression**, where the legal and **moral** rights of minorities are taken away. The examples in this book all show this cycle of prejudice. We will also see how attempts have been made to break the cycle of prejudice and enable the differences between people to make positive contributions to society.

Fear and persecution

Some people think that prejudice tells us more about the people who have it than it does about those who suffer its effects. It often grows out of fear or anxiety. We might say that prejudice is 'a feeling trying to find a reason'.

Many groups have been targeted in this way at different times. Ethnic minorities, women, the gay and lesbian communities, for example, have all had to suffer the effects of fear and anxiety about differences, and been the object of hatred, ill-treatment and even murder, simply because they were different from a powerful majority.

The language

of prejudice

Watch your language!

When we start to define people as though one thing about them was the whole truth, the way we speak about them, or even speak to them, changes. Everyday language is full of words that can be used to make people seem less valuable, important or human than they actually are. These words can be very insulting and hurtful and we should do everything we can to avoid using them, so that we do not give offence to others either deliberately or accidentally.

Racist language is a collection of insulting or abusive words that are based on the

Prejudice is concerned with looking at one characteristic of a person, eg skin colour, and defining that person as 'black' rather than 'human' with the same rights as everyone else. Slaves were given very few rights and certainly less than their, often white, masters.

belief that cultural or birth factors make one group of people superior to another. Sexist language reinforces the misguided belief that men are superior to women. Both racist and sexist language is very common. Sometimes it is deliberate, but often we use words and phrases that can cause offence without being aware of them, because they are so deeply embedded in our language and culture. We insult others when we reduce them to one (often imaginary) characteristic – the colour of their skin, the clothes they wear, their sexual orientation, and so on.

Don't just look at the black face.

Look at the whole person.

Sometimes the words and phrases that people use in their daily lives are less obviously racist or sexist than the insults we have just been looking at. For example, when somebody has a temper tantrum they may be described as 'being in a paddy'. It is often not realized that the word 'paddy' refers to an Irish person, as though fits of temper were the dominant characteristic of being Irish. Many Irish people find the phrase offensive. Can you think of other words or phrases like that?

Inclusive language

Again, many words and phrases used in more formal settings, such as the law, business and religion, are the products of institutional prejudice. They are long-standing, and almost unrecognized, assumptions about certain groups of people. For instance, all British laws speak of 'he' and 'him' rather than 'he or she' or 'him or her'. Although everyone accepts that both sexes are referred to in language like this, some people believe we should make much more effort to use inclusive language – ways of saying things that include both men and women equally. Very often, for instance, we can say 'they' or 'their', and sometimes you will see the word 'S/he' written down (it's not easy to say it!), meaning 'She or he'.

Finding the right word is not always easy. Traditionally, the person who is in charge of a meeting has been called the 'Chairman'. As more and more women took on that role, it became important to find a new word. 'Chairperson' was used for a time, but while accurate, it seemed to many people to be a rather ugly word. Many people and groups now simply use the word 'Chair' to refer to the man or woman who is responsible for the proper conduct of a meeting. The English language has been changing rapidly over the past few years with people making a conscious effort to exclude institutionally prejudiced words and phrases and include those that refer to all social groups.

POLITICAL CORRECTNESS

Inevitably, some people dislike the changes in the English language. They accuse those searching for more inclusive and less offensive language of being 'politically correct', or '**pc**'. They claim that the changes are quite unnecessary, and are being forced on us by minority groups. Is this a fair point, or is it just another example of prejudice? What do you think?

Media stereotyping

The media

Prejudices tend to be at their strongest when powerful groups – whether in the majority, such as white people in Britain, or the minority, such as white people in South Africa – feel threatened. The 20th century saw the **mass media** – newspapers, radio, cinema, television and the Internet – grow to become powerful manipulators and creators of public opinion. The first act of any **dictatorship** is to gain control of the television and radio stations. The overriding concern for any government is to try to get the media on their side.

You shouldn't believe everything you read in magazines and newspapers, but too many people do.

THE WAR IN THE FALKLAND ISLANDS

In April 1982 the British government declared war on Argentina over disputed territory (the Falkland Islands) in the South Atlantic. There was much controversy about the war, but the government was able to count on the support of some, at least, of the most widely-read national newspapers. *The Sun*, in particular, was strongly supportive of the government and during the conflict a number of headlines appeared, aimed at changing public opinion about Argentina. In fact, they created prejudice against the country that had now become Britain's 'enemy'.

Prejudice persuades by half-truth, feeds on ignorance and gains strength by belittling, and so the very word 'Argentinian' was soon reduced to 'Argie'.

Naval ships and troops were sent to the South Atlantic and Britain imposed an 'exclusion zone' in the waters around the Falklands, saying that any Argentinian ships found inside it would be attacked. On 4 May 1982, an Argentinian cruiser, the *General Belgrano*, which was outside the exclusion zone and apparently sailing away from the Falklands, was attacked by a British submarine, *HMS Conqueror*. It sank and 360 members of the *Belgrano's* crew died. The attack was controversial but *The Sun* newspaper's headline left no doubt whose side it was on. Above a photograph of the sinking ship, the headline proclaimed 'GOTCHA!'. Having created a prejudice against Argentina, the newspaper could now try to manipulate the British people's response to the sinking of the ship and tragic death of its crew. It encouraged them to think of it as a game. It was as though sinking a ship was no different from hitting a coconut with a ball at a funfair.

The sinking of the Argentine cruiser *General Belgrano* on 4 May 1982.

Prejudice works by reducing a complex person to one dominant characteristic, and then turns that into a **caricature**. The mass media can contribute to this by creating caricatures or **stereotypes** themselves and then reinforce them in our minds by constant repetition.

Of course, some people argue that prejudice is necessary in war time, when the lives of our own soldiers and sailors are at stake. But there have always been others who believe that prejudice is never acceptable – even at times of war. Manipulation of public opinion by the media happened not only during the Falklands War. During the Gulf War and the Kosovan conflict, Saddam Hussein and Slobodan Milosevic respectively became the objects of abuse and hatred. But there is a narrow line between truth, half-truth and prejudice, and media stereotyping is an important weapon in a government's armoury.

The mass media may reinforce other prejudices, too. The slow drip-feed of media stories can gradually turn public opinion against a social group as well as political opponents. Once more, people are reduced to things. Some popular newspapers regularly print pictures of half-naked women ('Page 3 girls'), turning women into objects of sexual fantasy. Notice how even the phrase belittles – Page 3 *girls*, rather than women. In the same way, South African whites have tended to refer to all black men, of whatever age, as 'boy'. The media can also reinforce prejudice against ethnic minority groups, or against gay men and lesbian women, by the way they present stories and by the language they use.

People with disabilities

In Britain the Disability Discrimination Act of 1995 says that a person has a disability if they have 'a physical or mental impairment which has a substantial and long-term adverse effect on their ability to carry out normal day-to-day activities'. The same Act says that it is illegal to **discriminate** against a person with a disability by giving them less favourable treatment because of that disability.

People with disabilities may have to use a wheelchair to get around, or have visual or hearing impairments, or suffer muscular weakness due to cerebral palsy, or have particular needs because they suffer epileptic fits or are diabetic. In the past, it has often been assumed that such people are defined by their disability – they *are* blind, deaf or diabetic. Changes in society have helped us to see that people may have a disability, which may create needs, but they are many other things too – boys and girls, sportsmen and women, wives, husbands, mothers, fathers, workers, old and young, members of ethnic minority communities – in other words, *people*. These changes are helping people to break out of the cycle of prejudice.

'See the person' – a British government advert attempting to raise our awareness of prejudices about people who have disabilities.

The medical model and the social model of disability

Traditionally, society has tended to see disabilities as deviations from normality, problems to be treated, or ignored. But as disabled people have themselves begun to make their voices heard, so this medical model has been overturned. Disabled people define disability as the constraints that society places on people with particular needs, the barriers that are put up and that prevent people from fulfilling their potential.

Sometimes these barriers can be very real. Wheelchair users may not be able to enter buildings where there are only stairs. They may find shopping difficult, or going to football matches almost impossible, because of steps and narrow passageways.

The barriers of disablility are constructed by society. Why should having to use a wheelchair stop someone from playing sport?

They need ramps and wide doorways. They need light switches, too, which they can reach. If you are not a wheelchair user, see if you can borrow one for a few hours, and test for yourself just how hard it can be to get around. People who are visually impaired may have difficulty using lifts unless there is a bell signal or a recorded message. They need talking books, or books translated into **Braille**, which have to be up-to-date if they are not to be disadvantaged in education or at work.

Other barriers are put up by assumptions and attitudes. Once more we can see how easily we can slip into defining a person by just one characteristic. People with disabilities can be very frustrated when they are not asked directly what they want or need – as though being deaf or in a wheelchair somehow disqualifies them from having their own opinions. Perhaps this can be summed up in the question asked of a disabled person's carer, 'Does he take sugar?' The answer of course is, 'Ask him yourself.' Think how angry you would be if nobody ever asked you what you wanted, but only spoke to those around you and asked them to decide for you.

The social model of disability is an important advance and may be a valuable model for understanding a whole range of prejudice. In this way of looking at the needs of people with a disability, the restrictions are not caused by the disability (the 'impairment') itself but by the denial of the means for people who have the disability to achieve their full potential. People with disabilities feel that they are often excluded from social, cultural, economic and political life. Often they are not asked what they need, and even if asked, their needs are often ignored, or given a low priority.

DISCRIMINATION

Legislation, such as the UK's Chronically Sick and Disabled Person's Act or the Disability Discrimination Act, is an attempt to break the cycle of prejudice by making discrimination illegal, and trying to create services to meet the needs of people with disabilities. But the law alone is not enough. Changes in society have to happen at every level, at home and school, at work and in the world around us.

Sexism

When the English 18th century aristocrat Lord Chesterfield wrote in a letter to his son that 'Women are only children of a larger growth', he was putting into words the attitude of men towards women in most societies for most of history. The overriding social norm has been **patriarchy** – the rule of men. Of course there were many influential women in history. Examples are Queen Elizabeth I, the 19th century novelists Jane Austen and Charlotte and Emily Bronte, and social reformers Elizabeth Fry and Florence Nightingale. However, these were exceptions in a man's world, which pronounced that 'a woman's place is in the home'. Many of the assumptions about women may come from a time when men and women had very different roles in society. But from the end of the 19th century, with the growth of women's education, demands for greater equality of opportunity could no longer be ignored. Women were first allowed to vote in Britain in 1918, and throughout the 20th century many of the more public inequalities were overcome. The role of women in the two world wars raised their practical status and changed many attitudes, but institutional and unspoken prejudice did not go away.

Germaine Greer is the author of many texts including the famous *The Female Eunuch* (1970).

WOMEN'S RIGHTS

As long ago as 1913, the great campaigner for women's **rights** Christabel Pankhurst wrote of 'the system under which a married woman must derive her livelihood from her husband' and claimed that: 'For generations, women have been very silent. It is now the turn of the men who have done all the talking to listen to what women have to say.'

Feminism

By the 1960s women in general were less reliant on their husbands economically. But the cycle of prejudice was still in place, and the world remained a man's world. In 1970 the Australian Germaine Greer published a famous book, *The Female Eunuch*, in which she showed how inequality and **discrimination** against women was fundamentally oppressive. She argued that, despite all the changes in the 20th century, women were still the objects of harassment, degradation and even hatred by men, and that women themselves were propping up the patriarchal system.

Sexism is one of the most difficult cycles of prejudice to break because it is fed by some of the most deep-rooted fears and anxieties. The 1970s and 80s saw more equality, and laws such as the Sex Discrimination Act were passed to reinforce it. In the 90s, however, popular culture and the **mass media** began to create and encourage 'laddishness'. Popular culture is now a man's world again, dominated by football and alcohol, and women are often seen as sex objects. Television 'sit-coms' such as 'Men Behaving Badly' are popular not least because they reinforce these **stereotypes**.

It is clear that some underlying sexist attitudes have not gone away, as seen in the enduring popularity of 'Page 3 girls' and the increase in domestic violence against women. Women may no longer gain their livelihoods from their husbands, but many are in low-paid and part-time work. They must often do this as the sole wage-earner in a family, while also having to bear the brunt of keeping the home and family going. How far this is the old rule of men (patriarchy) back again, and how far it is a new sort of sexual equality is difficult to say. What do you think?

Images like this can reinforce stereotypes of the relationship between men and women.

Homosexuality

For some people, there can only be one sort of intimate relationship, that between a woman and a man. For others, close and loving relationships between two men or two women are not only possible but quite acceptable. Few areas of prejudice raise such strong emotions as the question of **homosexual** relationships. For some people, gay men and lesbian women are wicked and dangerous. For others, they are people living with and responding to their own needs. If prejudice works by labelling people and then making them live according to the labels, by refusing to see them as complex human beings, then the attitude of many of those who condemn homosexuals is undoubtedly prejudiced.

Normal or abnormal?

Just as traditionally society has tended to see physical disabilities as deviations from normality, problems to be treated or ignored, so it has seen homosexuality in the same way. But more recently, many people have begun to believe that human sexuality is much more complex, and simple ideas of what is normal or abnormal are not very helpful. The relationships between people are too varied, too complex, for that.

Just as prejudices against other groups have created lurid fantasies about their dangers and what they get up to, so homophobia (the hatred of homosexuals) has led people to believe that gay men and lesbian women are similarly dangerous people who would stop at nothing in pursuit of their way of life.

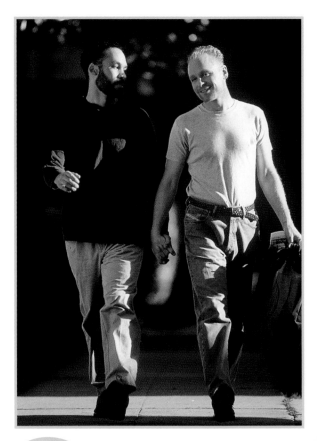

A male couple holding hands. Images like this make some people very angry. Other people believe that everyone should have the right to choose a partner and show their love.

Whatever you may feel, or come to feel, about people's sexual orientation, this sort of prejudice has no more basis in reality than the prejudices against Jews, women or disabled people. To accept that you are **heterosexual** or homosexual, has nothing to do with how you treat other people. Even if it is true that a majority of people are heterosexual, this does not mean that everyone must be, or that anyone who is not is abnormal. But attitudes to homosexuality are full of strong feelings and hard to overcome.

● *Although HIV/Aids was first identified in the gay community, it is certainly not a 'gay disease'. HIV/Aids is now a much greater killer of heterosexual people – in Africa, for instance – than of homosexuals. But the early presence of HIV/Aids amongst gay men has enabled a great many people to understand the difficulties for gay men of living in a society that has discriminated against them and often shown extreme prejudice towards them. The attitude of many heterosexuals towards gays has undoubtedly been changed by HIV/Aids.*

Schools

In 1988 the British government passed a law that effectively prevented schools from teaching young people about homosexuality in anything but a critical and negative way. Schools were not allowed to 'commend' homosexuality in any way. For many people, this law grew out of prejudice based on ignorance, although others believed, and still do, that because heterosexuality is 'normal', children and young people should be encouraged to accept this as their own way of life in adulthood.

In 2000 the British government proposed that this law be repealed and that schools should be allowed once more to speak about the homosexual relationship as one of a number of situations in which adults may choose to live. This proposal is still very controversial, but for many teachers and adults, as well as for many children and young people, relationships are about much more than sexual orientation. They are about the care and love with which people live together and treat one another. Relationships like this, many people say, can be either heterosexual or homosexual. The important thing is that we understand ourselves and learn to live with how we are.

A gay rights march demanding equality of opportunity and raising people's awareness.

Power and prejudice

We have defined prejudice as opinions we form about other people which help to justify our own anxieties or fears, and which are based on inadequate or distorted facts. We may look at other people, or groups of people, and realize that they are different from us. If we are comfortable with ourselves, then the fact that other people are different is unlikely to be a threat. But sometimes these differences do seem to be a threat – to our own way of life, our prosperity, or even our health. It is then easy to imagine that these 'different' people are the cause of our problems. It is a small step from there to deciding that they are 'abnormal' – not as fully human or worthy of respect as we think we are.

The cycle of prejudice

And so, the cycle of prejudice begins – inequality leads to **discrimination**, which in turn leads to **oppression**, and finally to **repression**, as the 'different' people are pushed further and further out of society. Refusing to understand them as complex people like ourselves, we turn them into **caricatures** – one-dimensional pictures – so that we can stop seeing them as people and turn them instead into objects.

Prejudice, then, is linked to power. Some governments use this tendency to fear or hate what is different as a way of creating repressive regimes. As the cycle of prejudice rolls round, so it reaches the point where governments may actually build laws into their national life that turn personal prejudice into systematic repression. **Rights** of whole groups to basic freedom and protection under the law may be denied on the grounds of ethnic origin, **gender**, sexual orientation or religious belief.

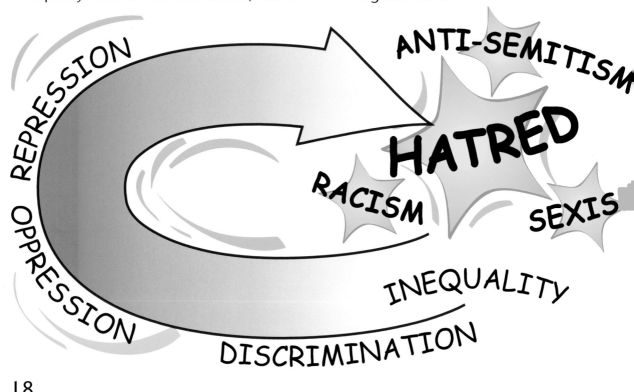

South Africa

In South Africa, the white community, which had become the most powerful during most of the 20th century, controlled the black population by laws of **apartheid** – literally, 'separateness'. This prevented any sort of relationship between the communities, except as rulers (whites) and servants (blacks). While the white community was generally wealthy, healthy and well-educated, the black community lived in shanty towns on the edge of the big cities, into which they had to travel to work as servants or labourers. Black children were badly educated and health care was very poor. The white population used their in-built political and economic power to prevent any change, and reinforced it by establishing a police state that crushed any opposition.

Gradually, though, things did change, under pressure from other countries and growing opposition from within. Finally, in the 1990s, with the release from prison of Nelson Mandela, a long-standing opponent of apartheid, the system crumbled very quickly. Free elections were held, Mandela became President of South Africa and the various apartheid laws were abolished.

The TRC

The problem facing South Africa, however, was how to deal with the aftermath of apartheid, what to do with the bad feelings left over when the cycle of prejudice had been broken. As power shifted from the white community to the black, there were fears that resentment would lead to revenge.

The way that South Africa dealt with this was by setting up the Truth and Reconciliation Commission. The TRC was a forum where those who had committed political violence, and their victims, came together to tell their stories. Chaired by Archbishop Desmond Tutu, it was a middle way between a trial and national forgetfulness. The many harrowing accounts of torture, imprisonment and murder were gathered into a single report, which revealed the complex responsibilities for violence in a state locked into the cycle of prejudice. But the TRC was not able to punish anyone. It recognized that both the white oppressors and the black victims were guilty of abuses of human rights, that in a world of deep-rooted prejudice there are no winners, and that it will take many years and much uncertainty before the wounds of prejudice can be healed.

Archbishop Tutu addressing the Truth and Reconciliation Commission (TRC).

Anti-Semitism
and ethnic cleansing

Anti-Semitism

Anti-Semitism, the conscious, systematic and deliberate hatred of Jewish people. It is often claimed to stem from the belief that Jews were responsible for the death of Jesus Christ, but is probably much older. The word 'anti-Semitism', however, was invented by Wilhelm Marr in the 1870s to refer to the opposition to Jews because of their social, economic and political status in the Germany of his day. Anti-Semitism is a deliberate attempt to remove **rights** to equal treatment from the Jewish people, to put Jews back inside social and geographical boundaries – **ghettos** – and to justify their ill-treatment by claiming that they are the enemies of the state.

From 1933 to 1939, Jews in Germany were systematically and deliberately discriminated against, oppressed and eventually **repressed** by being put outside the protection of the law. During those years 'Jews not wanted here' signs were put up in shops, cafés and by the side of roads. In October 1933, Jewish doctors were banned from hospitals. In September 1935, laws were passed which made Jews officially 'second class citizens'. In November 1938, German schools were closed to Jewish children.

The clearing of the Warsaw ghetto in Poland, 1943. The Jews were forced to leave at gunpoint by German soldiers.

FACT

● *Distorted ideas about Jews have been commonplace throughout Europe for centuries. Jews have been figures of fun and objects of fear. The character of Shylock in William Shakespeare's* The Merchant of Venice *is a good example, although Shakespeare shows more sympathy for the Jew than most of his contemporaries would have. But the cycle of prejudice against Jews culminated in the 20th century in the German Nazi party's systematic attempt to destroy the Jewish people.*

From 1939 to 1945, as Germany under Adolf Hitler dominated much of Europe, this repression turned into a programme of killing in which almost six million Jews died, while about 800,000 others escaped to countries outside German influence.

The power of this prejudice continues, however. Neo-Nazi groups (sympathizers with Hitler) are still strong in Germany and elsewhere in Europe, particularly where there are economic problems that can be 'blamed' on immigrants.

Anti-Semitism is a particularly terrible hatred that has lasted for centuries and taken many forms. But the 20th century saw many other attempts to destroy whole nations and communities.

Some Jewish communities, such as those of Eastern Europe, were vulnerable because they had no land of their own. After the Second World War, Jews were given the land of Israel as a home, but this could only be done by displacing Palestinian Arabs living in the same place. Jews and Palestinians have not found it easy to live together.

Ethnic cleansing

Nations sharing a homeland with others can be very vulnerable to shifts of political power. The conflict in the Balkans during the 1990s brought the phrase 'ethnic cleansing' into popular use. Ethnic cleansing is the systematic attempt by one national or religious group to destroy another. So, in the Balkan states of Serbia, Croatia and then Kosovo, minority groups were attacked and forced to leave their homes, and many of the men were killed. After attacks on Kosovan Albanians by the Serbian army, Western nations led by the USA and Britain used force to help protect them.

FACT

● *The Kurds are another people with no homeland. There are 22 million Kurds, most of whom are Muslims. They live in parts of Turkey, Iraq, Iran and Syria. Twenty per cent of the Turkish population and twelve per cent of the Iranian population are Kurds. Despite this, their rights have been ignored by the Turkish and Iranian governments, which have persecuted and at times systematically killed them.*

In 1999 these Kosovan Albanians, along with thousands of others, were forced to flee from Albania after the Serbian army carried out its policy of 'ethnic cleansing'.

Religious intolerance

Many of the conflicts between national groups are also examples of prejudice based on religious differences. Although many think that religion is much less important to people in the modern world, in fact the number of conflicts with a combination of political, ethnic and religious elements is increasing. Religious prejudice is built on half-truths about someone else's religious beliefs, which are used as an excuse for attacking them, hating them, even killing them. It has often been a major factor in conflicts and in ethnic cleansing or genocide (the systematic killing of a racial group simply because they are different). Although most world religions offer a message of peace, different religious groups still find it very difficult to live together.

Some followers of a particular religion say that they, and only they, have the truth. They sometimes go even further and say that other religions are not just false, they are also dangerous. They say they are like infectious diseases that have to be avoided, and even eradicated. Religion touches people's feelings very deeply, and intolerance to other people's beliefs is still common, even among people who do not go to church, mosque, synagogue or temple.

An Orange Lodge march in Northern Ireland. Members of the Roman Catholic community often find such displays offensive.

Sometimes differences are marked by what we wear.

Christianity, Judaism and Islam

Many religious differences go back many centuries and have become institutionalized prejudices that one group of people hold about another. Christian intolerance of Jews – anti-Semitism – is almost as old as Christianity itself, despite the fact that Jesus of Nazareth was a Jew, as were his first disciples. More recently, as Jews have begun to live close to Islamic countries – such as Egypt, Syria or Iraq – religious differences between Judaism and Islam have also helped fuel wars and distrust.

Intolerance does not only occur between the followers of different religions, but also between different groups within one religion. Conflict between Sunni and Shi'ite Muslims, for instance, has fuelled

PARTITION

In India, Hindu and Muslim lived together with reasonable toleration for centuries, but religious differences became a factor when the country gained independence from Britain in the 1940s. Politicians, under pressure from deeply committed religious people on both sides, agreed to 'partition' India into one mainly Hindu country (India itself) and two mainly Islamic countries (Pakistan and Bangladesh). In 1948, when independence finally came about, and despite the attempts of the great man of peace Mahatma Gandhi, there was much bloodshed when people of the 'wrong' religion were found on the 'wrong' side of the partition. Even today, there are often conflicts on the borders of India and Pakistan. Although they may be sparked off by territorial claims they also keep religious intolerance active.

war in the Middle East. In Northern Ireland, deep-seated prejudices between the different Christian groups there – Roman Catholic and Protestant – have been responsible for decades of civil unrest and killing.

One vision

Religious intolerance is very complex. People hold on to their religious beliefs with great determination, and who is to say they are wrong? But as we come to have a greater knowledge of the major world religions – Buddhism, Christianity, Hinduism, Islam, Judaism and Sikhism – we can begin to understand that they all have visions of wholeness, of one world living in peace. Perhaps this greater mutual understanding will help to overcome many different forms of prejudice in society. Schools are an important place for it to start.

Racism

Labelling

Just imagine what it would be like if someone came into your school classroom with a tape measure and a handful of labels, told you all to line up, measured your height, one by one, then, according to your height gave you a label to tie on your wrist. Now everyone with a label saying their height is under 1.3 metres is told to go and stand outside in the rain, they 'need to grow before they can be educated'. Everyone with a label saying '1.3–1.5 metres' is told to sit down and get on with their work. Everyone with a label saying 'over 1.5 metres' is told to go home – they are 'too tall to be educated'. Unfair? And yet this sort of labelling goes on all the time. We often give people labels based on one of their characteristics, in this case height, and treat them according to that label.

Stereotyping

Stereotyping happens when we think that just because someone has one characteristic they must have others. Let us say we assumed that everyone over 1.5 metres tall was lazy, supported Liverpool football team, and bit their fingernails. Prejudice happens when we create a whole set of values and beliefs based on these **stereotypes**. So everyone over 1.5 metres tall will probably not get a job because they are assumed to be lazy. **Discrimination** happens when these prejudices are built into society by people with power. So in this case employers might ask all applicants for a job to write their height on the form, and automatically reject everyone over 1.5

Harriet Tubman – a 19th century slave in Southern America. She escaped in 1849 and devoted her life to the causes of slave **emancipation** and women's rights.

metres tall. **Repression** is what happens when these characteristics form the basis for law. So no one over 1.5 metres tall would, in that case, be allowed even to apply for a job.

Racism is what happens when ways of labelling and stereotyping people according to their ethnic origin (which often in practice means according to the colour of their skin) become ways of discriminating and repressing whole social groups. Racism, then, is the result of prejudice plus power.

Like all prejudice, racism depends on half-truths, wrong and muddled beliefs that many people are not even aware they have until they are encouraged to think more carefully about what they say, and about their attitudes.

CHECKLIST FOR RACISM

Here are some typical racist attitudes – all of which need to be challenged.

Racism means…

- believing people from one group share characteristics – for example, 'All Chinese people gamble' or 'All West Indians like Reggae'

- hating people from ethnic minorities and trying to force them out of the country

- expecting ethnic minorities to fit into 'the British way of life'

- white people using their power to exclude black or Asian people from opportunities for good health care, education and employment

- doing nothing when white people call black or Asian people abusive names

- supporting fascist organizations like the British Movement

- blaming ethnic minorities for poor housing conditions or rising crime

- believing black or Asian people are inferior to whites – less intelligent, lazy, not capable of doing the same job

- believing that people from ethnic minorities with disabilities do not need services because 'their own people will look after them'

- black or Asian people hating whites or each other

After many years in prison, Nelson Mandela became the first black president of South Africa, and a great symbol of hope for oppressed people everywhere.

Racism in Britain

Slavery

There is a long history of the **oppression** of black people by whites. The slave trade, which was at its height in the late 18th and early 19th centuries, transported over 20 million people from Africa to the West Indies and to the southern states of America to work on plantations as the property of white landowners. The abolition of the slave trade in Britain and then in America, while ending this terrible practice, did not bring an end to **discrimination** and **repression**.

From Empire to Commonwealth

In the 19th century, the British Empire steadily grew until 20 per cent of the world's population was effectively ruled from London. This provided a huge (and predominantly black) workforce in Africa, the West Indies and India to produce cheap goods for Britain, and for trade with the rest of the world. Britain also moved vast numbers of people around the Empire. Indians were shipped to the West Indies and to Africa. South Sea islanders were taken to Queensland in Australia to work on sugar and cotton plantations. As the British Empire gave way to the '**Commonwealth**' and former colonies became independent once more, so the worldwide pattern of racism, in which white nations were the rulers and black peoples provided cheap goods and labour, began to be played out in Britain itself.

West Indian immigrants, like these at Southampton in 1956, came to Britain full of hope; for many the reality was to be very disappointing.

all have different
nily backgrounds
that doesn't mean
can't be friends.

Race riots

In the 1950s and 60s, **immigration** from the West Indies, and later from India and Pakistan, was encouraged by the British government. There were major labour shortages as Britain rebuilt itself after the war, and this New Commonwealth **migration** was important in providing people to work for low wages in unpopular jobs, such as in hospitals and transport. The numbers of immigrants grew – 60,000 arrived in 1960 and 120,000 in 1961. Communities were established in many towns and cities – especially Manningham in Bradford, St Paul's in Bristol, Brixton and Southall in London, and inner Leeds. But racial tension increased, and there were race riots in Nottingham and in Notting Hill Gate, London. Some white groups said that the newcomers were taking away jobs and diluting the 'pure' British nation (itself already a mixture of wave after wave of incomers – Celts, Romans, Saxons, Vikings, Normans, and so on).

There had, of course, been black communities in Britain for generations. Liverpool, for instance, had had one since the 1750s.

But the impact of the New Commonwealth migration after the Second World War was considerable, and created a multi-cultural Britain in which racial tension has been a major negative force. British racism started as British **imperialism**. The main function of black communities for Britain has been to provide a cheap work force, but they have not been given the same opportunities as white people. Black people make up only 5 per cent of the United Kingdom's population. However, over 50 per cent of the prison population is black and 40 per cent of the black population is unemployed. Although the 1976 Race Relations Act made it illegal to discriminate against someone because of their colour, race, nationality, national or ethnic origin, black communities argue that they experience discrimination every day of their lives. It is a part of their British experience.

FACT

● *In June 1948, an old troopship, the* Empire Windrush, *sailed into the port of London with 510 people from the West Indies on board. They were not allowed to land at first but eventually they did and were housed in a large, old air-raid shelter on Clapham Common before moving into houses in Brixton, which became the core of the Afro-Caribbean community in Britain. There was a lot of anxiety expressed by British people, who were worried about their jobs and disturbed by the prospect of mass immigration. A government minister, Arthur Creech Jones, tried to calm the panic by saying that the newcomers 'won't last one winter in England'. He believed that the immigrants would be forced back to their hot countries by the cold of an English winter.*

Institutional racism

Black people's experience of being undervalued and discriminated against every day of their lives cannot be ignored. The cycle of prejudice is like a wheel that moves round. **Inequality** leads to **discrimination**, **oppression** and **repression**, but this itself feeds a stronger sense of inequality. Beliefs, however wrong, that a group is inferior, or more likely to commit crime, get built into the way society organizes itself.

In recent years, many police forces have had a policy of recruiting officers from ethnic minority groups.

Black people and crime

Closed circuit television cameras can now be seen in most town centres, in car parks and on railway stations. It is claimed that they are an important weapon in the fight against crime. Recent research has shown, however, that the people who operate the cameras are more likely to track a young black man wearing a baseball cap, than a middle-aged woman. Is this because the camera operators are actively racist? Not necessarily. But they are acting according to a belief that young black men are more likely to commit crime than middle-aged women. Is that true? How can we really say?

Crime figures depend upon crimes seen and arrests made. If video cameras are busy tracking young black men, they may well catch some of them committing crimes. But they may miss the middle-aged white woman who is shop-lifting.

Many people have criticized the police for so-called 'Stop and Search' procedures, because black communities believe they are being unfairly targeted. Is this because the police are racist? Not necessarily. They may simply be responding to crime figures, which suggest that black men are more likely to carry weapons or be involved in crime. But if more black men are stopped than white, then it is more likely that more black men than white will be caught in criminal activity. It does not mean to say that more black men than white are actually breaking the law. How could they be, when 95 per cent of the population is white!

Stephen Lawrence

On 22 April 1993, two young black men, Stephen Lawrence and Duwayne Brooks, were attacked by a group of youths in South-East London. Stephen died from stab wounds. The police investigated the killing but were heavily criticized by Stephen's parents and others for their actions. The police did not treat the attack as racially motivated and were increasingly seen by the black community as full of 'racist prejudice, **stereotyping** and insensitivity', while the investigating team showed 'inappropriate behaviour and **patronizing** attitudes' to the dead young man's family. After many investigations into the circumstances not only of Stephen's death but also of the police investigation, a public inquiry was held. It concluded that the Metropolitan Police were 'institutionally racist' and that their attitudes had led to a failure to make a proper investigation of Stephen's killing.

WHAT IS INSTITUTIONAL RACISM?

The Stephen Lawrence Inquiry defined institutional racism as

'The collective failure of an organization to provide an appropriate and professional service to people because of their colour, culture or ethnic origin. It can be seen or detected in processes, attitudes and behaviour which amount to discrimination through unwitting prejudice, ignorance, thoughtlessness and racist stereotyping which disadvantage minority ethnic people.'

The Stephen Lawrence Inquiry pointed out that 'tight-knit organizations' like the police were likely to act in this way because the attitudes and behaviour of individuals reinforce prejudices. It is institutional racism that makes the wheel of prejudice go round.

Institutional racism, as defined by the Lawrence Inquiry, can be seen in many different aspects of British life – perhaps even in your school. We need to test our own attitudes towards others against it.

The parents of Stephen Lawrence.

29

Complex prejudice

Prejudice is not a simple thing, because inequality and **discrimination** work in many different ways. Prejudice becomes a powerful force in society when it feeds a range of anxieties. People may be worried about their jobs, or their health, and look for another group to blame for the problem. They may be worried about bigger social issues too. Some people argue that the discrimination against New **Commonwealth immigrants** in Britain was partly the result of British people recognizing that their country was less important in the world than it had been. Britain had ruled an Empire 'on which the sun never set' (it spread all around the world), but now that was disappearing fast. To make things worse, people from those countries were coming to take up work. It seemed not to matter that the New Commonwealth **migration** was to fill jobs that the local, white population did not want. What did matter was the threat, the change, the sense that things were 'not what they used to be'.

Prejudice and politics

Prejudice is a useful weapon for politicians too. Hitler was able to take power, and remain powerful for twelve years, through his vicious anti-Semitism that found a response among so many other Germans and Europeans.

The German Nazi party identified shops belonging to Jews – "When you see this sign… Jew". The shops could then be boycotted, or worse, attacked and robbed.

ENOCH POWELL

In the late 1960s the issue of immigration became important for the revival of Conservative politics in Britain. A high-profile Conservative, Enoch Powell, claimed in a speech that unless something was done about the tide of immigrants from the New Commonwealth, there would be massive racial violence. He said 'rivers of blood' would flow if these 'alien cultures' were allowed to 'swamp Britain'.

It was ironic that Powell should have made these remarks when it was he, as Minister of Health, who had encouraged immigration as a way of providing a cheap work force for the Health Service in the 1950s. But his purpose in making the speech was not simply to attack the black community. It was to use the prejudice against the black community to gain support for his vision of a racially and culturally pure England. This he could only do by creating an enemy – a force that could be claimed to be putting this Old England of thatched cottages and pretty villages at risk. Powell used the anxiety of the English worker about disappearing jobs to attack the black communities, and so establish support for his views. Nevertheless, he struck a chord. He received over 100,000 letters of support. By 1970 he had gone further – the black communities had become, for him, part of an 'enemy within', who along with students and others, were out to destroy Britain.

Positive contributions

People have seen in Enoch Powell's attack on black communities the way in which politicians can use anxiety and prejudice to gain power and influence. You can also see how complex prejudice can be – by subtle use of language, a politician can feed many anxieties and prejudices at once. In Powell's speeches, black workers are said to be destroying British culture and also making white workers unemployed. No mention is made of the way in which the black population was in fact being exploited, working for low wages, far away from their families and homeland, and in poor housing. No mention is made of just how hard it was to be a black person in London or Nottingham or Bristol. Neither did Powell speak of the positive economic and cultural contributions they were making, despite their hardships. Prejudice feeds on fear, and it also feeds fear – but only in a climate of untruth.

Enoch Powell, a British Conservative politician, helped create a climate of racial tension and prejudice by speaking against the growing black communities of the 1960s.

Ways of dealing with racism

All forms of prejudice can be very complex and there are no simple ways to deal with them. This is just as true of racism. But racism is a fundamental part of our society and needs to be challenged in ourselves and others. How can we do that?

Educating ourselves

If prejudice grows out of half-truths, unquestioned assumptions, thoughtless labelling and careless **stereotypes**, then one important step is to make sure that each one of us does all that we can to learn and understand about other people. We must treat other people as complex, interesting individuals, not just as objects or things. The society in which we live is complex and can be an exciting but challenging place to grow up in. Many prejudices become strong when we start to be afraid of those challenges. But what is there to be afraid of?

Challenge others

Prejudices tend to be shared. The Stephen Lawrence Inquiry said that institutional racism was able to flourish in the police force because it was such a closely knit organization. It can be very difficult to challenge prejudice when we see it in others – even harder than to challenge it in ourselves. But the experience of many people is that prejudices only start to fall away when they do challenge them. The more we know about other religions or cultures, and the more we understand and accept sexual equality ourselves, the easier it is not only to challenge other people's prejudices, but also to change their minds.

Rastafarianism

The Rastafarian movement is a religious organization dedicated to encouraging the self-reliance of the black community. It began in the slums of Jamaica in the 1920s. It was named after Ras Tafari – another name for Emperor Haile Selassie of Ethiopia – and Rastafarians believe that they will one day return to Africa. The strength of Rastafarianism has been its capacity to make its followers proud of their black inheritance and culture. Rastafarians mark themselves by wearing their hair in dreadlocks and by smoking ganja (marijuana), which of course is against the law and so leads to problems with the police. Many Rastafarians are also **vegetarians**.

Rastafarians feel pride in their black inheritance and culture.

Be proud

We have all been brought up to accept the existing power structures of society – a society that often defines itself now and in history as white, male and **heterosexual**. An important part of the process of freeing ourselves from those assumptions is to learn more about the group to which we belong, and to be proud of our own history. The members of every group affected by prejudice can learn this lesson, by finding role models, and by being determined to see the world from where they are and not from somebody else's point of view.

Martin Luther King – the champion of Civil Rights in the United States.

CIVIL RIGHTS

In 1955 a 14-year-old black youth was murdered in Mississippi because he was said to have whistled at a white woman. Emmet Till was drowned after having a heavy weight attached to his neck with barbed wire. There had been many such racist murders in America but Emmet's death focused the attention of many Americans, both black and white, on their country's treatment of the black community.

Out of his death, and under the leadership of a Baptist pastor, Martin Luther King, a non-violent civil **rights** movement grew up. It gradually won over politicians and many others. The protest took essentially peaceful forms, for example sit-ins and boycotts of

segregated public places (places where blacks and whites were not allowed to be together). But it was met with violence from the police and right-wing organizations.

In February 1962 President Kennedy presented a Civil Rights Bill to Congress. It failed, but one year later it was passed and over 250,000 people marched through Washington singing the song of the Civil Rights movement - 'We Shall Overcome'. Martin Luther King spoke to the crowd. 'I have a dream,' he said, '...of a nation where [people] will be judged not by the colour of their skin but by the content of their character.' King was assassinated in 1968 and his dream has still to become a reality – but his speech remains a stirring challenge to everyone to fight prejudice wherever it is found.

Difference is positive

Some people think that the world is divided up into two kinds of people. There are those who say, 'There is one way of looking at the world, one truth about life, and I know what it is.' And there are those who say, 'There are many true things in life, and I'm trying to find out what they are.' Prejudice starts from the first way of thinking about the world. To overcome prejudice we have to start being like those who never stop searching for the many true things.

Constant change

Ask yourself, 'What do I know about myself?' Earlier in this book there was a suggestion that you made a list, or a

Sport provides many important models for racial integration; all communities in a town or city can be proud of their football team.

drawing if that was better, to try to show all the many different things you are, and the many different relationships you have with other people. That is you. Now imagine we asked everyone you had put on your list of people to say something about you. They too would say many different things, some good, some perhaps bad, but would you recognize yourself in what they said? Perhaps. But you would probably also want to say that there were still things missing. Things about you nobody knows about, things

differences to just a few labels and make sure everyone is wearing one or another of them. They see differences as 'deviations from normality'.

Celebrating difference

Some people, however, love difference, which is why they are also the enemies of prejudice. They think that prejudice takes away the very thing that makes people interesting and valuable – the way they are different from each other. Prejudice makes the world dull and boring, as well as dangerous. Some people celebrate difference and do everything they can to encourage it and enjoy it.

about you that have changed, and things you want to change. So, if we are all changing all the time, it is hopeless to try to pin labels – either on yourself or on other people. The truth is, we never quite know ourselves, or anyone else, because we are always changing. That's what makes us human, and fascinating.

Keeping things the same

The people who want to pin things down to just one sort of truth do not like change either, and will do anything they can to prevent it. They do not like differences, and will do whatever they can to make it look as though everything is much the same (or at least can be put into a limited number of boxes). They need prejudice as a way of dealing with difference. Prejudice is a way both of accepting differences, but also of trying to pretend they are not there. Prejudice starts from the belief that 'I' am 'normal' and anyone who isn't pretty much like me is 'abnormal'; so 'man' is normal, 'woman' is 'abnormal'; 'sighted' is normal, 'blind' is 'abnormal' and so on. People with prejudices limit

WHAT ARE YOU INTERESTED IN?

Football? Music? Do you play a sport, or are you part of a youth theatre or an orchestra? Everything we do needs the contribution of different sorts of people, from different backgrounds. Professional football and cricket use the skills of players from many different cultures. Popular music wouldn't exist without the sounds of gospel singing and reggae. You can easily buy food from China, India, Pakistan or the Middle East in any town in Britain. Rap poetry, a wonderfully rhythmic style, is some of the liveliest around. Why not write some rap to celebrate the difference between people?

Human rights

What are rights?

The *American Declaration of Independence*, first published on 4 July 1776, said that 'all men are created equal, that they are endowed with certain inalienable **rights**, that among these are Life, Liberty, and the pursuit of Happiness.' Today we are used to saying that people have certain basic rights, but in 1776 this was quite a new idea.

Many people think that the cycle of prejudice effectively takes people's rights to 'life, liberty and the pursuit of happiness' away from them. The more society fixes labels on people, the easier it is to treat those people as less than fully human, and so to believe that they have fewer rights. Sometimes politicians have encouraged this, as an excuse for killing whole groups of people, sending them into slavery, or denying them proper housing, education or health care. As the cycle of prejudice spins around and prejudice turns to **discrimination** and **repression**, so laws may be passed to prevent these groups from sharing in the wealth and success of the country in which they live.

People who affirm universal human rights say that no one should be denied fair and just treatment just because of the colour of their skin, or their religion, or for any other reason.

Rights and responsibilities

Human rights are also about human responsibilities. Your right to equal treatment has to be balanced by your responsibility to treat other people as equals. At first, such rights and responsibilities were in practice limited to small groups. The American declaration did not prevent the appalling treatment of Native Americans, for instance. However, it was a

A copy of the American Declaration of Independence, 4 July 1776.

seed that would lead eventually to a great flowering of justice in the **emancipation** of slaves, the civil rights movement and the modern belief that discrimination on the grounds of sex, race or religion is unacceptable. It reached its most universal form in the United Nations Declaration of Human Rights of 1948, which stated:

'All human beings are born free and equal in dignity and rights... Everyone is entitled to all the rights and freedoms set forth in this Declaration, without distinction of any kind, such as race, colour, sex, language, religion, political or other opinion, national or social origin, property, birth or other status…' (from Articles 1 and 2).

The United Nations Declaration is a very important document, which tells us what we should all be aiming for, both in society and in ourselves. It is a fundamental attack on prejudice and a celebration of difference. But in many aspects it remains as words on a page, and is often ignored. Institutionalized prejudice – prejudice woven into the very fabric of society – can reinforce inequality, discrimination and **oppression**. We all have to care about human rights – because they are our rights too. And we have a responsibility to care about the rights of other people – treating them justly and fairly, not discriminating against them because of the colour of their skin, or their religion, or for any other reason.

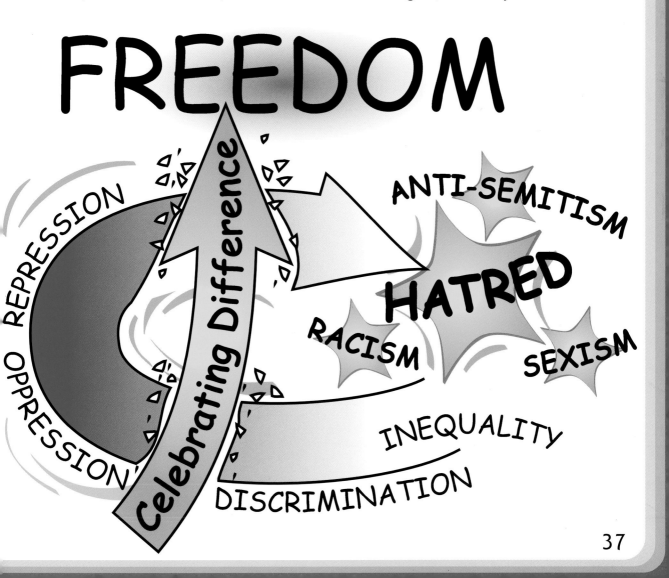

The rights of children and young people

Legally, anyone under the age of 18 is a child, although we usually call older children 'young people'. The United Nations Convention on the Rights of the Child starts from the belief that children and young people need special protection because they can be very vulnerable; that they should all be treated with the same care; and that anything that adults do for them or to them should be in the best interests of the children and young people themselves.

Countries that agree to abide by the United Nations Convention must have laws which make sure that children:

- have proper health care and access to education
- are protected from work that is dangerous or will prevent them from being healthy and properly educated
- are protected from abuse or **exploitation**, and especially sexual exploitation or prostitution.

Many of the world's children live in terrible conditions, with no medical care or schools nearby. The UN Convention was written to try and protect children from such hardship.

Prejudice

Some people can be very prejudiced against children and young people. There is an old saying that 'children should be seen and not heard', which suggests that a lot of older people think children should just do what they are told, accept what happens to them, and not argue. But young people are increasingly having their say. As long ago as 1911, some school children went on strike in protest about the way they were being treated. Today, many schools have councils in which young people and their teachers discuss things about their school and come to agreements about some aspects of school life that may need changing.

Children must be protected from exploitation like this.

In some countries it is illegal for parents to smack their children. This is not yet the law in Britain, although the UN Convention on the Rights of the Child thinks it should be. However, many kinds of physical punishment are now banned and against the law in Britain.

Working children

For centuries children and young people were exploited. They were made to work down mines, in the fields or as chimney sweeps, for long hours and in terrible conditions that shortened their lives. In some countries today, children are still made to work at dangerous jobs. In the UK, however, there are tight regulations about the sort of work school-age children can do. They cannot work, for example, in any place where food is cooked or where heavy machinery is used.

Responsibilities

Children's rights go alongside responsibilities. The United Nations Convention is clear that the best place for children and young people to develop into confident adults is within their own families. Children and young people may be protected by law from ill-treatment inside or outside their families, but they are expected to behave responsibly towards themselves and their carers.

Does your school have a policy about children's rights? What do you think it should include? When adults have to make decisions about children and young people, they are expected to balance what they think a young person needs with what that young person wants. How would you make that balance for yourself? How would your class, tutor group or year do that? Would things be any different from the way they are now?

The law in the United Kingdom

The United Nations Declaration on Human Rights has led to many laws being passed to try to remove the worst effects of prejudice and to try to make sure that all parts of society have **equality** of opportunity.

Speaking out about racism – a Childline poster.

Children and racism - A ChildLine study

The following Acts of Parliament have been passed in the UK:

• The Sex Discrimination Act (1965) – It is against the law when at work, in education, or providing any goods or services, to discriminate directly or indirectly between men and women. At work it is also illegal to treat married people less favourably than single ones.

• The Race Relations Act (1976) – It is unlawful to discriminate against someone on the grounds of their colour, race, nationality, national or ethnic origin. This applies to white people as well as black, to Gypsies and Jews, and citizens of other member states of the European Community.

• The Equal Pay Act (1970) – There must be equal pay and conditions of work for both men and women doing work of equal value when working for the same employer.

• The Disability Act (1981) – Local authorities and those responsible for road building must take the needs of disabled and blind people into consideration when building roads. It also says that appropriate signs should be provided to help people with disabilities.

- The Disability Discrimination Act (1997) – Anyone who provides a service to the public must also provide suitable access to those services for people with disabilities. This does not just mean ramps to replace stairways, but also suitable literature and appropriate telephone facilities for the hard of hearing, for instance. An organization called the Centre for Accessible Environments has produced an 'Access Audit Pack' showing how to create safe environments for people with a range of disabilities.

Prevention better than cure

A former Secretary General of the United Nations, Boutros Boutros Ghali, has said that 'it is easier and cheaper to prevent war than to end war once it has started'. The same could be said of prejudice. The many laws that try to give equality of opportunity to everyone in society are important, and a great advance on the situation even 30 years ago. But laws alone do not defeat prejudice and bring about equality of opportunity. That can only happen when you are determined to treat everyone around you as an equal – and to enjoy the many differences which make our society so rich in opportunities and insights.

It's against the law to refuse to interview me for a job just because I'm black.

It's against the law to pay me less than a man for doing the same job.

What can I do?

A lesson for us all

A German Christian minister, who was later to be a victim of Hitler's Nazis, once wrote:

First they came for the Jews,
and I did not speak out
  Because I was not a Jew.
Then they came for the communists,
and I did not speak out
  Because I was not a communist.
Then they came for the homosexuals,
and I did not speak out
  Because I was not a homosexual.
Then they came for the trade unionists,
and I did not speak out
  Because I was not a trade unionist.
Then they came for me
  And there was no one left to speak for me.
                              (Martin Niemoller)

Look around you

Prejudice – whether in our attitudes to black people, gays, women or those with disabilities – is a complex thing. It is deeply embedded in our society, and has an effect on every aspect of it – work, education, health, sport and leisure. Despite the changes in the law, and the shift in people's attitudes, many difficulties still remain. Young people may be stopped and searched by the police and be convinced it was just because they were black. People may be badly treated at work because they are women, or black, or disabled in some way. Footballers can be the subject of racial abuse if they are black or from a foreign country. People with disabilities may be denied access to leisure facilities because,

Chains brought to England by David Livingstone to show slavery was still continuing in East Africa.

for instance, there is no ramp into a building, or a swimming pool has no hoist to help them get into the water.

Speak out

When we ask what we can do, the problem may just seem too big. Would it

42

not be better just to say nothing? Just to try to live our own lives? But, as Martin Niemoller saw, by saying nothing we can make things worse. The cycle of prejudice may begin just with inequality, but it soon moves on to injustice and **oppression**, and can end with **repression**, for example slavery, the **Holocaust** and ethnic cleansing. On the small scale it makes people unhappy and undervalued. On the large scale it kills.

Get involved

Many people decide that they can make a difference by getting involved with clubs or organizations that work to overcome prejudice and celebrate difference. Human **rights** organizations, such as Amnesty International, have many campaigns in which young people can take part. A lot of schools have their own branch of Amnesty International. If your school doesn't, you might like to start

one. You might even want to start a club that tackles problems of racism or sexism in your school or neighbourhood. Other organizations support people with disabilities, campaigning for proper facilities.

Break the cycle

We all have a responsibility to live according to the United Nations Declaration on Human Rights – to treat people with respect, dignity and fairness, and as equals. You have a responsibility to do whatever you can to challenge prejudice wherever you see it. This can be very difficult, but the more we understand the rich variety of life our society has to offer, and how the many different groups we live among contribute positively to our world, the easier it can be to break the cycle of prejudice, first of all in ourselves, and then in others.

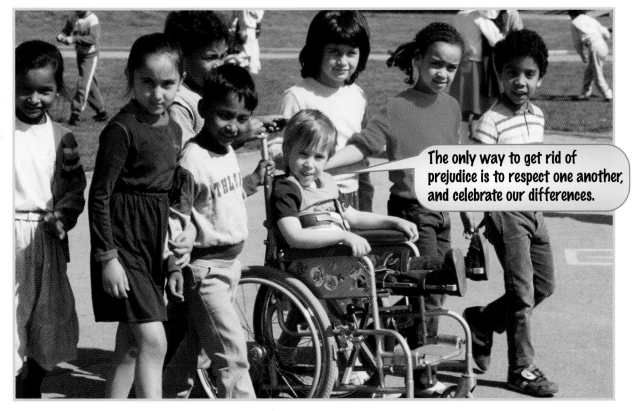

The only way to get rid of prejudice is to respect one another, and celebrate our differences.

Glossary

apartheid a political system in which different races are kept apart; especially associated with South Africa under white rule

Braille a form of raised type that enables blind people to read texts by touch

caricature an exaggerated or ridiculous picture of someone

Commonwealth a large group of countries which were once ruled by Britain, which have now formed a looser association for trade and cultural links

dictatorship a country ruled by the power of a single person, whose word is law and who ruthlessly prevents any opposition

discrimination favouring some people over others; not treating everyone equally

emancipation the act of setting free; can refer to slaves, women or any other group of people who are oppressed

exploitation using someone for selfish purposes; for example, making children work for very low wages

gender the sex of a person, either male or female

ghetto originally the part of an Italian city where Jews lived. During the Second World War, the part of a city or town where Nazis confined Jews before taking them to concentration camps. It can now mean that part of a town or city where an identifiable racial group live which they may find hard to leave, or be prevented from leaving.

heterosexual being sexually and emotionally attracted to someone of the opposite sex

Holocaust the mass murder of Jews by the Nazis during the Second World War

homosexual being sexually and emotionally attracted to someone of the same sex

immigration to move into a country to live and work there

imperialism the policy or practice of a country extending its rule over other countries, dominating them politically and economically

mass media the forms of communication that reach large numbers of people, such as newspapers, magazines, television, the internet and radio

migration the movement of people from one place to another

militant using violence or active protest to change things

moral the kind of behaviour that you, or other people, think is right and fair

oppression preventing some groups of people from having access to such things as healthcare, education or good jobs

patriarchy a form of society in which men have all the power and women have none

patronizing looking down on someone as less important

pigmentation the colour of someone's skin

repression using laws to take rights away from some groups in society

rights those things we share in a just society: such as the right to go to school and be educated; the right not to be abused or exploited; the right to be treated the same as everyone else

segregation a policy, law or process that separates one racial, ethnic or religious group from the rest of society

stereotypes ideas we have of people which stop us seeing them as individuals

superficial refers to the surface of things; we have superficial attitudes to things and people when we haven't thought much about them

vegetarian someone who believes that not only is it wrong to eat meat, it is also unhealthy

Contacts and helplines

AMNESTY INTERNATIONAL
99–119 Rosebery Avenue
London, EC1R 4RE
020 7814 6200 – Campaigns on human rights issues.
www.amnesty.org.uk

CHILDLINE
Freepost 1111, London N1 0BR
0800 400 222 – 24-hour helpline. Children can phone or write with a problem of any kind.
www.childline.org.uk

THE COMMISSION FOR RACIAL EQUALITY
Elliott House, 10–12 Allington Street
London, SW1E 5EH
London *020 7828 7022*
Edinburgh *0131 226 5186*
Cardiff *029 2038 8977* – Works to stop racist behaviour and support protection laws.
www.cre.gov.uk

NSPCC (National Society for the Prevention of Cruelty to Children)
National Centre, 42 Curtain Road
London, EC2A 3NH
020 7825 2500
Child Protection Helpline: *0800 800 500*
cinni.org/nspcc

PHAB (Physically Handicapped and Able Bodied)
Summit House, 50 Wandle Road
Croydon, Surrey, CR0 1DF
Many towns and schools have PHAB clubs where young people with physical disabilities can meet with other young people on equal terms. Write to PHAB Ltd for the address of your nearest club.

THE UNITED NATIONS CONVENTION ON THE RIGHTS OF THE CHILD
can be downloaded from UNICEF's Voices of Youth website at
www.unicef.org

THE UNITED NATIONS UNIVERSAL DECLARATION OF HUMAN RIGHTS
can be downloaded on
www.hrw.org/hrw/universal.html

IN AUSTRALIA

HUMAN RIGHTS AND EQUAL OPPORTUNITY COMMISSION
Level 8, Piccadilly Tower
133 Castlereagh Street
Sydney
NSW 2000
2 9284 9600

KIDS HELPLINE
1800 551800

REACH OUT
www.reachout.asu.au
Helps children with a variety of problems

Further reading

Fiction

Dangerous Skies
Suzanne Fisher Staples
HarperCollins, 1998

From the Notebooks of Melanin Sun (Point Signature)
Jacqueline Woodsun
Scholastic, 1997

The Storyteller's Beads
Jane Kurtz
Gulliver, 1998

What if the Zebras lost their Stripes
J Reitano
Paulist Press, 1998

Non-fiction

Anne Frank: Beyond the Diary
R van der Rol (ed.)
Puffin, 1995

The Diary of Anne Frank
Penguin, 1997

Neo-Nazis - A Growing Threat
Kathlyn Gay
Enslow, 1997

We Are Witnesses: Five Diaries of Teenagers who Died in the Holocaust
Jacob Boas (ed.)
Scholastica, 1996

Index